Trauma-Informed Teaching: From Reaction to Restoration

A Healing-Centered Approach
for Homeschool Cooperatives and Microschools

Dr. Annise Mabry

Trauma-Informed Teaching: From Reaction to Restoration

A Healing-Centered Approach
for Homeschool Cooperatives and Microschools

Dr. Annise Mabry

Dedication

For every student who was told they were too much,
too broken, or too far behind.

You are not the problem.

You are the possibility.

About The Author

Dr. Annise Mabry is a nationally recognized edupreneur, strategist, and community impact architect. Long before edupreneurship became a buzzword, Dr. Mabry was developing a homeschool-based business model that defied conventional thinking and changed the lives of thousands in the process.

As the founder of The Dr. Annise Mabry Foundation and Tiers Free Academy, she pioneered a trauma-informed, diploma-granting homeschool cooperative that has served over 6,000 families and issued more than 1,000 high school diplomas to students who were left behind by traditional education systems.

A trusted expert in grant writing and sustainable program development, Dr. Mabry has secured millions of dollars in federal, state, corporate, and foundation-level grants to fund education, mental health, and workforce programs in rural communities. Her unique ability to merge community needs with entrepreneurial innovation has positioned her as a leading voice in the edupreneurship movement.

Today, she mentors emerging edupreneurs, nonprofit leaders, and grassroots changemakers by helping them turn their passion into profitable, community-rooted solutions.

TABLE OF CONTENTS

Prologue

When I first started the Tiers Free Homeschool Cooperative, it began as a small Facebook group. It gave me a way to connect in real time with new homeschool parents stepping into this space while supporting children with learning differences or special needs. What started as a point of connection soon became something much bigger.

Then, when I started my nonprofit organization, I moved the homeschool cooperative under the nonprofit as a program. As the community latched on, it quickly revealed itself to be something far more expansive. But it was so much more than just a program. It was a lifeline for thousands in rural communities all over Georgia. I built it from the ground up as a trauma-informed, community-powered alternative for students who had been pushed out, passed over, and broken down by traditional systems. It was funded by grants that recognized the importance of what we were doing: offering academic restoration, emotional safety, and a pathway to a high school diploma for youth who had nowhere else to turn.

But in 2025, everything changed.

We lost over $100,000 in grant funding in a matter of weeks. No warning. No plan B. Just gone.

When that happened, I realized something important. The crisis was not limited to funding alone. It extended to our sustainability, our strategy, and our ability to weather uncertainty. I was no longer leading a program. I was carrying the weight of an entire community on my shoulders. A community that was counting on me to figure it out.

This is my pivot. It's my real-time response to funding loss, burnout, and the deep grief of watching something you built be threatened by forces beyond your control. But it's also a guide for every homeschool leader, every microschool founder, every nonprofit educator who knows what it means to be needed more than they're resourced.

I originally wrote this book for education changemakers working in homeschool cooperatives and microschools. As I began sharing it with beta readers from more traditional education settings, I realized its reach extended far beyond that original audience. This book speaks to a diverse community of educators, leaders, and caregivers who are committed to creating safe, healing-centered learning environments. That includes K–12 teachers, homeschool facilitators, school counselors, social workers, and district leaders supporting students impacted by trauma, exclusion, or systemic barriers. It also resonates with alternative education providers, including professionals working in juvenile justice and reentry programs. Additionally, it supports college faculty, teacher preparation programs, afterschool mentors, and parents or caregivers seeking compassionate, effective strategies for emotionally impacted or neurodiverse learners.

Whether you teach in a classroom, around a kitchen table, or within a correctional facility, we share a common mission: to move beyond behavior management and restore dignity, trust, and purpose to every student's educational journey.

I wrote this book and built the online course to give you a framework, one that centers regulation over rigor, restoration over reaction, and healing over hustle. When the grants run out, the mission still has to stand.

This is my most vulnerable work. It's transparent. It's raw. It's real. And it's proof that even in the middle of the storm, we can still teach. We can still lead. We can still pivot toward purpose.

—Dr. Annise Mabry

xiii

Trauma-Informed Teaching: From Reaction to Restoration

A Healing-Centered Approach
for Homeschool Cooperatives and Microschools

Chapter 1

THE NEW LEARNING LANDSCAPE

WHY TRAUMA-INFORMED TEACHING BELONGS IN HOMESCHOOL COOPERATIVES

"We cannot heal in the same environment that hurt us. We can, however, learn in one that truly sees us." —Dr. Annise Mabry

INTRODUCTION: A SHIFT IN WHO TEACHES AND HOW LEARNING HAPPENS

In living rooms, church basements, and small storefronts across the country, an educational revolution is quietly taking shape. Parents, educators, and community leaders are building learning environments that reject one-size-fits-all schooling in favor of flexibility, connection, and care. These spaces are not traditional classrooms, and they are not constrained by rigid bureaucracy. They are homeschool cooperatives and microschools, and for many trauma-impacted youth, they are the first places where learning finally feels safe.

Homeschool Cooperatives and microschools aren't automatically trauma-informed. Just because a learning space is small doesn't mean it's automatically trauma-informed. If we're not careful, we recreate the very systems our students were running from. That is why trauma-informed teaching is not optional. It is essential.

THE RISE OF HOMESCHOOL COOPERATIVES AND MICROSCHOOLS

Over the past decade, the face of education has changed. COVID-19 accelerated what many families were already feeling: the traditional school system wasn't working for their children, especially those who are neurodivergent, emotionally sensitive, or living with complex trauma. As a result, we've seen an explosion in alternative models like:

- **Parent-led homeschool cooperatives**, often rooted in community or faith values
- **Microschools** with mixed-age classrooms and personalized learning
- **Online/offline hybrid pods** that blend digital curriculum with in-person connection

These models offer flexibility, but they also come with responsibility. Many leaders of these spaces have never received formal training in trauma-informed education, yet they are tasked with supporting students who carry heavy emotional and behavioral burdens.

Why Trauma Shows Up Differently in Cooperative Settings

In traditional schools, trauma can be masked by structure. But in the close-knit environments of co-ops and microschools, it shows up more raw and unfiltered:

- A child shuts down during a group activity
- A teen lashes out during a math lesson
- A parent seems overbearing or combative during check-ins

These are not behavior problems. They are survival responses. Without the ability to recognize them, we risk punishing what should be healed.

In trauma-informed homeschool settings, we learn to ask different questions:

"What happened to you?" instead of "What's wrong with you?"

"What do you need to feel safe?" instead of "Why can't you follow the rules?"

THE ROLE OF THE EDUCATOR AS HEALER, NOT JUST TEACHER

Homeschool cooperative leaders wear many hats. You're a guide, a facilitator, a mentor, and often a surrogate parent figure. Trauma-informed teaching doesn't mean becoming a therapist—it means becoming a consistent, regulated adult who models calm, compassion, and curiosity.

In this new learning landscape, the trauma-informed educator must be:

- **Predictable**: Creating routines that reduce anxiety

- **Empathic**: Understanding that behavior is communication

- **Flexible**: Adapting expectations without lowering standards

- **Connected**: Prioritizing relationships over rigid rules

FROM REACTION TO RESTORATION

Too often, when trauma shows up, we respond through punishment, withdrawal, or frustration. Trauma-informed teaching invites us to choose restoration instead.

It asks us to restore a sense of agency for the learner.

It asks us to restore trust in adult relationships.

It asks us to restore hope that learning can still feel joyful and safe.

Perhaps most importantly, it calls us to restore ourselves as educators who are often carrying vicarious trauma, burnout, and self-doubt.

CASE STUDY: NIA'S STORY

Nia was 14 when she joined a homeschool cooperative after being expelled from her local middle school for "disruptive behavior." At the co-op, she would walk out of lessons, shout at peers, or stare blankly for hours. Her facilitator, a former public school teacher, wanted to help. Instead, she defaulted to strict rules and escalating consequences, and nothing worked.

It wasn't until the co-op team received trauma-informed training that things shifted. They learned to recognize Nia's silence as dissociation and her anger as fear. Instead of sending her home, they asked what she needed. They offered choice, structure, and non-punitive reflection.

Six months later, Nia was leading a project on environmental justice and mentoring younger students. Her trauma didn't disappear, but she now had a place to learn without fear.

THE URGENCY OF NOW

If we want homeschool cooperatives and microschools to serve as true safe havens, not merely academic alternatives, trauma-informed teaching must be the foundation of our work rather than an afterthought. This is not about lowering standards. It is about raising humanity.

This is the moment to build something different. This is the moment to teach from restoration.

Chapter 2

RECOGNIZING TRAUMA

WHAT HOMESCHOOL LEADERS NEED TO KNOW

"When we see a child's behavior as the problem, we miss the story behind the behavior. But when we learn to read the signs, we can begin to teach through healing." —Dr. Annise Mabry

INTRODUCTION: TRAUMA DOESN'T ALWAYS LOOK LIKE TRAUMA

Not every child who has experienced trauma will scream, cry, or act out. Some will become the quietest in the room. Others will become the funniest. A few will seem like natural leaders. Trauma doesn't have one face—it wears many masks.

As homeschool leaders, it's easy to assume trauma "belongs" to someone else's classroom, and that we'll be spared the hardest stories because our spaces feel smaller, safer, or more intentional. Yet trauma often walks right through our doors anyway, carrying truths that won't stay hidden. It rarely announces itself on new student applications or fits neatly into check boxes on enrollment forms. Instead, it slips into our learning spaces quietly, takes a seat, and waits for someone to notice what it has been carrying for far too long.

To be trauma-informed is to first become trauma-aware. This chapter explores the many forms trauma can take, how it shows up in homeschool settings, and what every cooperative leader should look for before responding to behaviors that are misunderstood far too often.

DEFINING TRAUMA: BEYOND THE OBVIOUS

Trauma is not just about what happened to a person. It is about how their brain and body experienced that event. What feels overwhelming and life-altering to one student may not even register for another. The key factor is whether the experience exceeded the child's ability to cope.

Trauma can be:

- **Acute:** a single event, like a car accident or sudden loss

- **Chronic:** ongoing abuse, neglect, or instability

- **Complex:** multiple, layered traumatic experiences

- **Collective:** community or generational trauma, such as systemic racism, displacement, or poverty

Many homeschool families come to cooperatives because their child experienced trauma in traditional settings, including bullying, discrimination, academic exclusion, or school-based policing.

But trauma can also live quietly behind the curtain:

- A parent's incarceration

- Food insecurity

- Witnessing domestic violence

- Medical trauma or chronic illness

- Foster care placement

- Emotional abandonment

Recognizing trauma begins with unlearning the myth that "traumatized kids" look a certain way.

RECOGNIZING TRAUMA RESPONSES IN REAL TIME

The learning environment may change, but the nervous system doesn't forget. Most trauma responses fall into four categories (fight, flight, freeze, or fawn). These will be referenced throughout the book, so here's a brief, practical snapshot:

As we'll revisit in later chapters, these trauma responses are survival strategies, not discipline problems.

1. Fight

Behavior: Verbal outbursts, defiance, physical aggression

Mini-Narrative: Malik, 13, throws a pencil across the room after being asked to redo a worksheet. This is not an act of disrespect. His nervous system experienced the correction as a threat to his sense of worth.

2. Flight

Behavior: Avoidance, wandering, zoning out

Mini-Narrative: Lily, 9, often "forgets" to bring her journal and asks to go to the bathroom during group reading. This is not disinterest. It is a response to feeling overwhelmed by the fear of making a mistake.

3. Freeze

Behavior: Silence, blank stares, inaction

Mini-Narrative: Carlos, 11, shuts down during math and remains silent for the rest of the lesson. The difficulty was not the question itself. It activated memories of humiliation from his previous school experience.

4. Fawn

Behavior: Excessive compliance, people-pleasing

Mini-Narrative: Naomi, 14, always helps clean up and nods at every suggestion. She never asks for help, even when she is struggling. Pleasing adults has become her safety strategy, one she relies on to avoid being sent away.

Curiosity over correction is gold.

When we lead with curiosity, we replace punishment with possibility. Every behavior becomes a clue.

WHAT HOMESCHOOL LEADERS OFTEN MISS

Because homeschool environments are often more flexible, trauma signs can slip through the cracks. Some red flags may be disguised as "helpful" or "quiet" behaviors:

- A student always volunteers to clean but never wants to read aloud

- A teen becomes the "helper" instead of doing their own academic work

- A parent avoids communication or appears overly controlling

- A child is compliant but struggles with comprehension

- A student resists transitions even when they appear calm

These are not quirks. They are cues that require attunement rather than assumptions.

TRAUMA IS NOT AN EXCUSE—BUT IT IS AN EXPLANATION

Being trauma-informed does not mean lowering expectations. It means changing how we respond when students are dysregulated.

Ask yourself:

- Is this student trying to avoid something that feels unsafe?

- What need is this behavior trying to meet?

- How can I offer support without reinforcing fear?

In trauma-informed education, we discipline through relationship, not removal.

WHEN TO REFER OUT: RED FLAGS FOR DEEPER SUPPORT

You are not expected to be a therapist. But you are expected to recognize when professional support is needed. Recommend a trauma-informed mental health provider if a student:

- Talks often about harm, violence, or death

- Expresses thoughts of self-harm or suicide

- Has severe mood swings or aggression

- Regresses developmentally in sudden ways (e.g., bed-wetting)

- Displays concerning changes in hygiene, eating, or sleep

Homeschool cooperatives thrive when they are part of a larger care network.

WHAT YOU CAN DO NOW

You don't need a certification to be a healing presence. You just need to:

- Pay attention to what students aren't saying

- Assume every student benefits from trauma-informed practices

- Prioritize connection before content

- Lead with curiosity over correction

A trauma-informed cooperative is not defined by its curriculum. It is defined by a culture of care.

TRAUMA AWARENESS AS A LEADERSHIP PRACTICE

To lead a trauma-informed homeschool cooperative is to recognize that learning cannot begin until safety is felt. This chapter is your foundation. As we discussed in Chapter 2, trauma responses show up in many forms, and the rest of this book will help you meet them with strategy, compassion, and courage.

Restoration is not limited to hospitals or counseling centers. It can also take place in homeschool basements, in group circles, and at the kitchen table.

Restoration happens with people who believe healing belongs in education.

Chapter 3

FROM PUNISHMENT TO PURPOSE

RETHINKING DISCIPLINE IN MICROLEARNING SPACES

"You can't punish pain out of a child. You can only love safety into them." —Dr. Annise Mabry

INTRODUCTION: WHEN RULES HURT INSTEAD OF HEAL

Most of us were taught to equate discipline with control, which looked like clear rules, consistent consequences, and zero tolerance. These structures often feel safe for adults because they create the illusion of order; but when we apply traditional discipline models to children who have experienced trauma, we often escalate the very behaviors we are trying to correct. Instead of restoring safety, we reinforce fear, and the child retreats, shuts down, or pushes back even harder.

Homeschool cooperatives and microschools are uniquely positioned to do things differently. Free from rigid policies and bureaucratic red tape, these learning spaces have the freedom and the responsibility to shift from punishment to purpose.

Discipline should not be about compliance. It should be about connection, reflection, and restoration.
That's what trauma-informed discipline looks like.

WHY TRADITIONAL DISCIPLINE FAILS TRAUMA-IMPACTED LEARNERS

In many public and private schools, discipline follows a familiar pattern:

- Rule broken

- Consequence assigned

- Repeat if necessary

This transactional approach assumes that behavior is a choice made with full self-awareness and control. But trauma interrupts that ability. A child who has experienced trauma is often operating from the survival brain, not the thinking brain. They may not even remember what they did or why they did it.

In traditional settings, this can lead to a cycle of exclusion:
MISBEHAVIOR → SUSPENSION → MISSED LEARNING → FRUSTRATION → MORE MISBEHAVIOR

In homeschool cooperatives, it might look like:
DEFIANCE → SENT HOME → DISCONNECTED FROM GROUP → SHAME → AVOIDANCE OR ESCALATION

In both cases, the result is the same: the child becomes the problem instead of the pain being understood.

THE PURPOSE OF DISCIPLINE IN A TRAUMA-INFORMED COOPERATIVE

Discipline, in its original form, means *"to teach."*

In a trauma-informed homeschool setting, discipline should help a student:

- Understand what happened

- Reflect on how it impacted others

- Rebuild trust with the group

- Practice a better choice next time

This doesn't mean abandoning boundaries. It means shifting our approach to:

- Prioritize restoration over removal

- Focus on skill-building instead of punishment

- Recognize behavior as a form of communication, not defiance

WHAT PURPOSEFUL DISCIPLINE LOOKS LIKE IN PRACTICE

1. REGULATE FIRST, THEN REFLECT

DEFAULTING TO REGULATION BEFORE REFLECTION IS GOLD.

Before a student can reflect on their actions, they must feel safe. If they are dysregulated (crying, yelling, or withdrawn), logic and reasoning won't work.

Try:

- "Let's take a break and check in again in five minutes."

- "You're safe here. I'm not upset, and I'm not sending you away."

- Offer quiet time with sensory tools, music, or a movement break.

2. USE CONNECTION AS CORRECTION

REFRAMING DISCIPLINE AS CONNECTION INSTEAD OF CONTROL IS MASTERFUL—AND IT WORKS.

When students feel like the adults around them are safe and invested, they're more likely to want to repair ruptures.

Try:

- "What do you think we need to do to make this right?"

- "That behavior was not okay, but you are not in trouble. You are in learning."
- "Help me understand what you needed in that moment."

3. Replace Consequences with Restorative Practices

Rather than punish students, guide them toward making amends.

Examples:

- A student who disrupts group time helps lead the next activity.
- A child who hurt someone writes a note, draws a picture, or participates in a restorative circle.
- A student who breaks materials helps repair or replace them.

REAL-LIFE RESTORATIVE MOMENTS: WHAT'S POSSIBLE

Example 1: The Fight That Didn't End in Expulsion

Two students got into a physical altercation over a group project. Instead of removing both students from the co-op, the facilitator gathered the group in a restorative circle the next day. The students took turns describing what triggered the fight, how it felt, and what they needed going forward. One student admitted, "I thought if I didn't act tough, people would think I was weak."

The circle ended with a group agreement and a plan to create safe communication signals when tensions rise. Both students stayed and became accountability partners for each other.

Example 2: The Silent Shutdown

A teen completely shut down during an open discussion on family dynamics. He left the room, curled up in a corner, and wouldn't respond.

Rather than pushing him to talk, the facilitator simply sat nearby and said, "I'm here when you're ready." She returned later with art supplies. He eventually drew a picture instead of speaking, and that became his first step back into class.

Connection over compliance gave him the safety to re-engage.

DISCIPLINE SCENARIOS IN HOMESCHOOL COOPERATIVES

Scenario 1: The Disruptive Learner

Jayden interrupts constantly during lessons. The facilitator asks him to leave the room. He returns more agitated each time.

Trauma-Informed Shift:

The facilitator sets up a regulation corner with fidgets and calming visuals. Jayden is coached to use a "quiet pass" when he feels the urge to interrupt. Instead of removal, Jayden is offered tools to stay engaged.

Scenario 2: The Withdrawn Student

Aria shuts down every time she's asked to present in front of others. She's marked as "non-participatory."

Trauma-Informed Shift:

Aria is invited to present one-on-one with a peer first. Her participation is scaffolded with supportive feedback and alternative ways to show mastery. The goal becomes building trust, not forcing compliance.

SETTING BOUNDARIES WITHOUT BREAKING RELATIONSHIPS

Some homeschool leaders worry that being trauma-informed means being too lenient. This approach does not remove accountability. It reframes it.

Healthy boundaries are:

- Clear but flexible

- Rooted in relationships, not rules

- Repaired when broken—not used as grounds for banishment

A trauma-informed cooperative sets the tone with these guiding phrases:

- "In this community, we work through hard things together."

- "We don't have to agree, but we do have to be kind."

- "You're still a part of this group, even when you make mistakes."

WHAT TO DO WHEN YOU FEEL TRIGGERED AS A LEADER

Educators bring their own trauma histories, and a child's behavior can unknowingly trigger unhealed parts of ourselves.

If you find yourself reacting emotionally:

- Step away momentarily and ground yourself

- "Is this about the student, or is this about something inside me?"

- Model calm for the group: "I need a moment to think about how to respond with care."

Trauma-informed teaching isn't just for students.

It is a culture of collective restoration and you are part of that culture too.

THE DISCIPLINE WE CHOOSE SHAPES THE WORLD WE BUILD

In this chapter, you've learned that discipline in trauma-informed homeschool settings must be intentional, relational, and restorative.

You are not just managing behavior; you are shaping how children learn to resolve conflict, navigate big emotions, and feel connected to a community.

YOU ARE NOT HERE TO CONTROL STUDENTS.

YOU ARE HERE TO TEACH THEM HOW TO REGULATE, RELATE, AND RESTORE.

That's discipline with purpose.

That's trauma-informed education.

Chapter 4

SAFE SPACES START AT HOME

PHYSICAL, EMOTIONAL, AND PSYCHOLOGICAL SAFETY IN HOMESCHOOL LEARNING

"A classroom does not have to be in a school building to feel unsafe. It also does not need a school bell to be a sanctuary."
—Dr. Annise Mabry

INTRODUCTION: SAFETY IS THE FIRST CURRICULUM

Before a child can absorb a lesson, complete a worksheet, or engage in a discussion, they must feel safe. Safety in these spaces is not just physical. It must also be emotional and psychological. In homeschool cooperatives and microschools, where learning spaces may be family homes, church rooms, or living rooms turned classrooms, creating safety is both more possible and more essential.

Unlike traditional schools with metal detectors and mandated drills, homeschool educators have the flexibility to center comfort over compliance and belonging over behavior charts. That freedom also brings a challenge. How do we design safety in places that were not originally designed for learning?

This chapter explores how to make trauma-informed homeschool environments that help students feel seen, soothed, and supported—from the moment they walk through the door.

THREE TYPES OF SAFETY EVERY LEARNING SPACE NEEDS

In trauma-informed education, safety is not a buzzword. It is a baseline. It comes in three layers:

1. Physical Safety

This is about the environment itself: Is the space clean, predictable, and free from danger?

Key elements:

- Consistent layout (furniture and supplies stay in the same place)
- Soft lighting and reduced noise levels
- Access to water, snacks, and bathroom breaks
- A quiet area to practice mental wellness reset

Trauma Tip: Many trauma-impacted students are hypervigilant. Even small environmental changes can feel threatening. Giving advance notice of changes or letting students help rearrange spaces can build their sense of control.

2. Emotional Safety

This means students feel accepted, respected, and unafraid of humiliation, punishment, or rejection.

Key elements:

No yelling, sarcasm, or shaming

Mistakes are treated as learning, not moral failure

Conflict resolution prioritizes empathy over blame

Rules are co-created and rooted in community values

Trauma Tip: Trauma teaches children that people can't be trusted. Consistent emotional tone from facilitators helps rebuild that trust.

3. Psychological Safety

This refers to a student's internal sense of belonging, autonomy, and value.

Key elements:

- Students can voice concerns without fear
- Diverse identities and family structures are affirmed
- Choice is built into learning (e.g., how to demonstrate understanding)
- Students are asked what they need, not just told what to do

Trauma Tip: Students who've been silenced or ignored elsewhere need repeated opportunities to reclaim their voice. That might mean using journals, art, or check-in surveys to help them express themselves.

DESIGNING THE PHYSICAL ENVIRONMENT FOR SAFETY

Your learning space doesn't need to be Pinterest-worthy; it needs to be peace-worthy.

Consider these questions:

- Are there cozy corners with cushions or blankets for overwhelmed students?
- Do students know where to go or what to do when they feel anxious?
- Are sensory tools available (fidgets, noise-canceling headphones, weighted items)?
- Are transitions between subjects and activities smooth and clearly signaled?

Pro tip: Create a "Regulation Station" stocked with calming tools and labeled visuals. Teach students how to use it proactively, not just when they're melting down.

ESTABLISHING EMOTIONAL SAFETY THROUGH ROUTINES

Children from traumatic backgrounds often find comfort in predictability. Homeschool settings can capitalize on this by creating consistent daily rhythms.

Sample rhythm for a cooperative setting:

1. Morning check-in circle

2. Academic block 1

3. Movement/snack break

4. Academic block 2

5. Community project or life skills activity

6. Closing circle with highs/lows or affirmations

Routines give students a sense of control. They reduce anxiety and help prevent behavior issues before they start.

Keep in mind: Unexpected changes are sometimes unavoidable. When they happen, narrate them with care. "We usually go outside after math, but today it is raining. Let's do indoor yoga instead to help our bodies stay regulated."

CREATING A CULTURE OF PSYCHOLOGICAL SAFETY

Psychological safety is rooted in **relationships and respect**. Kindness alone is not enough. We must be intentional.

Here's how to build it:

- **Normalize feelings:** Post emotion charts and use feelings check-ins daily.

- **Honor privacy:** Let students opt out of public speaking or group activities when needed.

- **Invite reflection:** Ask students how rules feel to them, not just if they're following them.

- **Use inclusive language:** Avoid phrases like "real family," "normal," or "you should already know this."

- **Remember:** A trauma-impacted student may not trust you just because you're kind. Trust is built through repair, consistency, and time.

- **What to Do When Safety Breaks Down**

- Even the most loving environments will encounter conflict, fear, or dysregulation. The key is how we respond:

- **Name it without blame:** "It looks like something didn't feel safe for you just now. Let's figure it out together."

- **Regroup, don't reject:** Avoid sending students away as the default response. Instead, invite them to reset and return when ready.

- **Model co-regulation:** Show them how you calm your body and mind. "I'm going to take three deep breaths because I feel overwhelmed."

- **Reflect as a group:** After incidents, ask: "How can our community feel safer next time?"

Safety isn't broken by mistakes. It's broken by disconnection. When we lead with repair, we lead with love.

YOU ARE THE SAFE SPACE

Trauma-informed homeschool teaching is not just about what is on the walls or written into the schedule. It is about who you are when a child is in crisis.

- Your regulation helps them regulate.

- Your tone helps them feel respected.
- Your presence tells them, "You are safe here, even on your worst day."

In this chapter, you've learned that safety is not a strategy. It's a culture.

And that culture starts with you.

Because when we teach from a place of restoration, we create learning spaces that don't just educate.
They heal.

SAFE SPACE CHECKLIST

Use this quick-check guide to make sure your learning space supports emotional safety and regulation.

1. Regulation Station Ready?

Is there a designated calm corner or Regulation Station that students can access without stigma?

2. Calming Tools Available?

Are fidgets, sensory items, breathing visuals, or art supplies accessible for self-regulation?

3. Visual Reminders of Belonging?

Do you have clear signage that reinforces: *"You still belong, even when you struggle"*?

4. Curiosity Over Correction?

Do you pause to ask *"What's behind this behavior?"* instead of defaulting to punishment?

5. Emotional Check-ins Built In?

Is there time each day or week for students to name and share how they're feeling?

6. You Lead By Example?

Have you modeled your own regulation strategies so students see calm in action?

A trauma-informed space doesn't require perfection—just *intention* and *consistency*.

Chapter 5

HEALING-CENTERED LEARNING

STOP MANAGING AND START HEALING

"You can't teach a child to dream if their nervous system is still stuck in survival. Healing has to come first."

Let me say this loud and clear. Trauma-informed education is not a buzz-word. It is a lifeline.

When I created my first homeschool program, it wasn't because I had some big dream of becoming a homeschool pioneer. I built it because I was trying to save my child's life. I watched a system break her down, punish her pain, and push her so far to the margins that she nearly disappeared.

Healing-centered learning saved us both.

So, if you're leading a homeschool cooperative, a microschool, or teaching your own children at the kitchen table, this chapter is your heart check. It's your permission slip to throw away every toxic rule, outdated structure, and classroom trauma you might still be carrying around in your own teacher toolbox.

This is where we stop just managing behavior and start healing the learner.

HEALING-CENTERED VS. TRAUMA-INFORMED: WHAT'S THE DIFFERENCE?

Let's break this down:

- **Trauma-informed** asks, "What happened to you?"

- **Healing-centered** says, "What's possible for you—now that you're safe?"

Trauma-informed teaching recognizes the pain. Healing-centered learning restores the potential.

You don't just want to understand your student's trauma. You want to give them tools, experiences, and relationships that help them move through it.

- Healing-centered learning:

- Shifts the focus from *reaction* to *recovery*

- Treats every lesson as an invitation to reconnect with self-worth

- Makes joy and curiosity part of the curriculum

HEALING-CENTERED VS. TRAUMA-INFORMED: WHAT'S THE DIFFERENCE?

TRAUMA-INFORMED TEACHING	HEALING-CENTERED LEARNING
Asks: 'What happened to you?'	Asks: 'What's possible for you now that you're safe?'
Focuses on understanding trauma and its effects	Focuses on restoration, growth, and post-traumatic possibility
Responds to triggers with empathy and boundaries	Designs learning that fosters identity, joy, and future-building
Builds safety and predictability	Builds belonging, purpose, and vision
Teaches around the trauma	Teaches through the trauma, toward transformation

THE THREE ANCHORS OF HEALING-CENTERED LEARNING

In my work with students across every kind of story and circumstance, from traditional homes to foster care, from juvenile court involvement to school dropout, from newly arrived families to LGBTQ+ youth, I have found that healing-centered learning is held together by three anchors.

1. IDENTITY SAFETY

Students need to feel like they don't have to shrink, hide, or code-switch to be accepted.

Ask yourself:

- Do my materials reflect the diversity of my students?
- Do I use inclusive, affirming language?
- Can students see themselves in the classroom *without apology*?

Healing Tip: Replace "What do you want to be when you grow up?" with "What kind of life do you want to create?" That question hits differently.

2. EMOTIONAL ACCESS

Students need permission to feel and to process.

This doesn't mean turning your co-op into a therapy group. It means making space for emotion in the learning process.

When I taught my daughter to write poetry, I wasn't just teaching language arts. I was helping her find her voice again after trauma tried to take it.

Try this:

- Use a feelings check-in before starting lessons
- Let students journal or draw when they can't find the words

- Teach emotional vocabulary alongside your academic content

Healing Tip: Regulate yourself before responding. A dysregulated adult cannot co-regulate a child. Period.

3. Purposeful Learning

Healing-centered learning ties every lesson back to something meaningful.

Ask:

- How will this help my student understand the world better?

- Does this lesson affirm their strengths or remind them of their failures?

- Am I just checking boxes, or am I helping them build a life?

DESIGNING A HEALING-CENTERED HOMESCHOOL DAY

Although structure helps trauma-impacted students feel safe, it must be flexible enough to leave room for healing. A healing-centered day might include:

Morning Rhythm:

- Grounding moment (music, meditation, or gratitude circle)

- Connection check-in

- Flexible learning blocks with choice-based activities

Afternoon Rhythm:

- Movement or sensory-based activity

- Project-based learning or real-world problem solving

- Community circle or reflection time

Healing doesn't come from perfection. It comes from rhythm, relationship, and repair.

WHAT HEALING LOOKS LIKE IN REAL LIFE

Sometimes healing isn't a big dramatic breakthrough. Sometimes it's a student who used to hide under the table raising their hand.

It is a child who was expelled for "noncompliance" finally being able to say, "I do not understand. Can you help me?"

It's the moment a parent says, "I've never seen my child smile during a lesson before."

Healing looks like:

- Reduced outbursts
- Improved focus
- Rebuilt trust
- Resurrected joy

It is quiet at first, but once it appears, it spreads.

WHAT GETS IN THE WAY OF HEALING?

Let me be honest. These are the biggest blockers I see:

- Adults who aren't ready to release control
- Shame-based discipline practices
- Unaddressed educator trauma
- Pressure to "look academic" over being relational
- Curriculum that wasn't designed with healing in mind

Healing-centered education is disruptive. You will have to unlearn what you were taught about what "school" should look like.

But guess what? You're not just running a school.

You're building a sanctuary.

YOU ARE A HEALING-CENTERED EDUCATOR

If you've made it to this chapter, I already know who you are. You are someone who believes in love as part of learning, in futures that are not limited by the past, and in healing that can only grow within a supportive community. In a world that keeps asking kids to "fix their attitudes," you are the one asking, "How can I hold space for your healing?"

That's what makes you different.

That's what makes your homeschool cooperative or microschool sacred.

That is what makes you dangerous to every system that ever tried to break our children.

Now let's teach like restoration is possible, because it is.

Chapter 6

RESTORATIVE LANGUAGE

HOW WE TALK TO (AND ABOUT) OUR STUDENTS

"Language can be a wound or a window. In trauma-informed spaces, we speak to restore, not to control." —Dr. Annise Mabry

Let me tell you something that changed how I show up as an educator: **The words we speak to our students become the voice they carry inside.** If we're not intentional, we can become another echo of the voices that broke them. And I don't know about you, but I didn't come this far to become another adult who teaches through shame.

When you lead a homeschool cooperative or microschool, your words matter more than your curriculum. Your tone shapes the learning climate. Your feedback becomes their self-talk. Your correction becomes their confidence or their fear.

Restorative language is how we teach, heal, and hold space at the same time.

LANGUAGE IS A TOOL OF POWER

Let's be honest. Schools have historically used language as a tool to control students.

"You're being disruptive."

"You know better."

"I'm not going to argue with you."

"Because I said so."

In trauma-informed learning spaces, we do not use language to dominate.

We use language to connect. To regulate. To repair.

Restorative language doesn't mean you stop correcting behavior. It means you correct without humiliating. You redirect without rejecting. You name harm without naming a child as the harm.

FROM SHAME-BASED TO STRENGTH-BASED

Most of us were raised with shame-based language.

"You're too sensitive."

"You never listen."

"You're just lazy."

Maybe it worked well enough to keep us in line, but it came at the expense of our worth, our curiosity, and our trust in adults.

Here's how we shift:

INSTEAD OF THIS...	SAY THIS INSTEAD...
"What's wrong with you?"	"What's going on for you right now?"
"You're making bad choices."	"Let's figure out what support you need to make a better choice."
"That's not how we act here."	"That behavior doesn't match who you are in this community."
"You need to calm down."	"I'm here. Let's breathe together."
"You're fine."	"It's okay to feel what you're feeling. I've got you."

This is not about being soft. It is about being strategic. Language that respects the nervous system works better and builds trust that lasts.

THE WORDS WE USE *ABOUT* STUDENTS

Let's talk real for a minute.

The labels we use when speaking about students, especially when they are not present, shape how we treat them. They also shape how others treat them.

"He's just difficult."

"She's always lying."

"That one's got issues."

These phrases may seem small, but to a child who already feels broken, they become confirmation. Your team hears them too, and before long that language spreads through the culture of your learning space.

In a trauma-informed cooperative, we don't label students. We label behaviors.

There's a big difference between:

"He's manipulative," and "He's trying to get his needs met in the only way he knows how."

"She's lazy," and "She's overwhelmed and shut down."

"They're always looking for attention," and "They're looking for connection."

When you change your language, you change your lens. As your lens changes, everything you view through it begins to shift.

RESTORATIVE RESPONSES IN REAL TIME

Here are some practical examples of restorative language in action:

SCENARIO 1: A STUDENT REFUSES TO DO WORK.

Traditional: "You're being disrespectful."

Restorative: "Looks like this assignment is feeling hard right now. Want to talk about it or take a break?"

SCENARIO 2: A CHILD PUSHES ANOTHER DURING GROUP TIME.

Traditional: "We don't hit! Say you're sorry!"

Restorative: "Let's take a breath. Can you tell me what happened? Then we'll help you both repair this."

SCENARIO 3: A TEACHER TELLS A PARENT THEIR CHILD IS "OUT OF CONTROL."

Traditional: "Your child is disrupting the classroom learning."

Restorative: "We're seeing some behaviors that are signaling distress. Let's work together to figure out what your child needs to feel more supported."

TEACHING STUDENTS TO USE RESTORATIVE LANGUAGE

You're not just modeling restorative language—you're teaching it. Give students the tools to repair, reflect, and respond with care.

Try this:

- Teach sentence stems like:

    "I felt ___ when ___ happened."

    "Next time, I'll try to ___."

    "What do you need from me right now?"

- Create a "Conflict Toolkit" with phrases and prompts for peer repair.

- Use circle time or group dialogue to reflect on language: What does respect *sound* like? What does care *sound* like?

Healing-centered learning means we teach communication, not just content.

WHEN YOU SLIP—BECAUSE YOU WILL

Let's be real. You will raise your voice. You will say something reactive. You will forget to breathe first.

That doesn't make you a bad educator. That makes you a human.

The most trauma-informed thing you can do in those moments?

OWN IT. REPAIR IT. MODEL ACCOUNTABILITY.

Try:

- "That wasn't the tone I meant to use. Let's try that again."

- "I was feeling overwhelmed. I'm sorry for how that came out."

- "You didn't deserve to be spoken to that way. Let's talk."

Every time you repair, you show students how to repair. You teach them that adults make mistakes and also make things right.

THE POWER OF YOUR VOICE

Your voice is a tool of restoration.

Use it to disarm fear.

Use it to name dignity.

Use it to pull students closer when the world has taught them to expect rejection.

When you change how you speak to students, you change how they speak to themselves. That is how healing begins. In your homeschool cooperative or microschool, every word is a seed. When you plant restoration and water it with care, healing becomes possible.

Chapter 7

COMMUNITY MATTERS

PARTNERING WITH PARENTS AND CAREGIVERS

"If we want to heal the child, we have to heal the whole house-hold. Healing isn't just for the student. It's for the circle they come from." —Dr. Annise Mabry

WE CAN'T TRAUMA-PROOF CHILDHOOD, BUT WE CAN BUILD A HEALING COMMUNITY

You can build a trauma-informed community that protects a child's dignity and keeps their story from becoming their identity.

That work does not stop with the student. It often begins, and sometimes breaks down, with the adults who love them most.

If you are running a homeschool cooperative or microschool, you are not just teaching children. You are walking alongside families.

Some of those families are carrying grief.

Some are navigating court cases.

Some are exhausted and terrified that they are failing their child.

Some are simply trying to survive the week.

Trauma-informed education doesn't just happen in your classroom.

It happens in your conversations, your communication, and your compassion for the caregivers.

NOT EVERY PARENT SHOWS UP THE SAME WAY

Let's get this out of the way:

Not all caregivers are warm, communicative, or "easy to work with."

Some will be overbearing.

Some will be checked out.

Some may even trigger something in *you*.

That's not because they don't care.

It's often because they've been conditioned by systems that punished them, dismissed them, or labeled them as the problem.

Some are still healing from their own school-based trauma.

Some don't trust anyone who holds a clipboard.

That's why we lead with curiosity over criticism.

Instead of asking, "Why don't they come to meetings?"

Ask, "What barriers might be preventing them from showing up safely?"

A TRAUMA-INFORMED LENS ON CAREGIVER BEHAVIOR

WHAT YOU SEE	WHAT MIGHT BE HAPPENING
Defensive or combative attitude	Fear of being judged or blamed
Over-involvement or micromanaging	Anxiety from past school trauma
Silence or avoidance	Shame, overwhelm, or untreated mental health struggles

What You See	What Might Be Happening
Inconsistent follow-through	Housing insecurity, job instability, or caregiver burnout
Distrust of your program	History of broken trust with educators or institutions

We don't excuse harmful behavior. But we do contextualize it, so we can respond instead of react.

From that understanding, we build **bridges**, not walls.

RESTORATIVE COMMUNICATION WITH PARENTS

Trauma-informed educator-family relationships are rooted in:

- Respect

- Transparency

- Non-judgmental presence

Use "we" language:

- "Let's figure this out together."

- "We're on the same team here."

- "What would feel supportive to your child right now?"

Start with strengths:

- "He lit up during the science project. His creativity was on full display."

- "I noticed how gently she helped her classmate today. That kindness matters."

Most parents only hear from schools when something is wrong. You set a new tone by leading with what's right.

AVOID DIAGNOSING OR SHAMING:

Traditional: "Your child has anger issues."

Restorative: "We've noticed that your child is having a hard time managing big emotions, especially when they feel overwhelmed or frustrated. We're here to support them in developing healthy ways to express what they're feeling, and we'd love to partner with you on strategies that work both at home and in school."

LIVED EXPERIENCE: *WHEN THE SYSTEM SAID 'NEVER BRING HER BACK'*

After my daughter was severely bullied in public school, she was offered a scholarship to a private school.

Everything in me said it wasn't the right fit, but I gave in to the voices that said homeschooling wasn't "real" education.

From day one, she was seen as a problem. She was "an only". The only African American student in her classroom. The only student in the school from a single-parent home. The only student who didn't have a family with deep historical roots in the community.

She never did anything right.

The school's staff became her judge, jury, and unsolicited therapist.

And then one day, they called and said:

"Come pick her up. Never bring her back. This isn't working for us."

That was not just a dismissal. It was a declaration.

A declaration that my daughter, brilliant, sensitive, and creative, was unworthy of their space.

Once again, it became my job to fix what another system had broken.

That was the day I chose restoration over rejection.

That was the day I decided to build what didn't exist:

A homeschool cooperative where **restoration was the curriculum**.

That was 2012. I have been holding space for restoration ever since.

CREATING SAFE SPACES FOR CAREGIVER VOICE

A healing-centered cooperative doesn't just serve students.

It honors families as co-healers.

Here's how:

- Monthly "connection calls" instead of formal parent-teacher conferences

- Listening circles where parents talk without being talked at

- Language-accessible materials and translation support

- Cultural respect in curriculum and communication

- Problem-solving that starts with "What's going on?" instead of "What did you do?"

When parents know their voice matters, even when they don't have the words, they begin to trust the process.

WHEN THE HOME ENVIRONMENT *IS* THE TRAUMA

Let's talk about something that is hard.

Sometimes the trauma is not just around the child. It is inside the home.

This reality can feel impossible. You want to protect the student, but you may not be a mandated reporter, and you may not have access to the systems that intervene

Here's what you *can* do:

- **Document** patterns, behaviors, and concerning language

- **Offer resources**—not solutions (e.g., mental health contacts, food pantries, parenting workshops)

- **Be a consistent, regulated adult** they can count on

- **Don't over-identify or try to rescue**—just hold the space

You can't fix the home.

But you *can* be the one place where the child feels seen, heard, and safe.

WHEN A CAREGIVER IS DISRUPTING THE COMMUNITY

Let's be real sometimes, it's not the student, but a parent who is *actively* derailing the cooperative's culture.

Maybe they gossip.

Maybe they lash out in group chats.

Maybe they bring chaos instead of calm.

When that happens, you don't need to tolerate harm in the name of being "inclusive."

You can set boundaries with compassion and clarity.

Sample Boundary-Setting Language:

"I care about your child and your voice in this space. But I also have to protect the culture of our community. Let's schedule a one-on-one conversation."

"I'm noticing some tension, and I want to address it respect-fully. We don't allow disrespectful language in our shared communication."

"It's important that this remains a safe space for all families. If something isn't working for you, let's find a solution offline."

"You're always welcome here, but only if we're all committed to mutual respect."

Boundaries are not rejection. They are clarity with love.

CREATING A FAMILY-CENTERED COOPERATIVE CULTURE

Trauma-informed co-ops don't just *talk* about inclusion.

They design for it.

Try:

- Family orientation sessions that teach trauma-informed practices
- Weekly affirmations sent home with students
- "Home & Heart" assignments focused on storytelling and legacy
- Joy-centered family projects—not just compliance tasks
- Parent workshops on topics like co-regulation, emotional safety, and nervous system care

Let families lead, too.

Invite their wisdom into your structure.

CO-HEALING IS THE GOAL

When I say healing-centered learning is a community effort, I mean it.

No child heals in isolation.

No caregiver thrives without support.

No educator sustains without relationships.

Stop trying to fix families.

Start walking beside them.

Hold space for the hard things.

Celebrate the small wins.

Be the first adult who does not blame the parent for what the system caused.

When the family is seen, the child feels safe.

That is how restoration truly begins.

Chapter 8

REGULATION BEFORE RIGOR

PRIORITIZING EMOTIONAL READINESS

"You can't teach a dysregulated child. You can't reach them with logic, rewards, or rigor. You reach them by helping them feel safe in their own body first." —Dr. Annise Mabry

Let me say this plainly. Emotional regulation is not a soft skill. It is a survival skill.

If you are trying to teach a child who is dysregulated, disconnected, or in distress, it does not matter how strong your curriculum is. They will not learn a thing.

In traditional classrooms, academic rigor is king, with deadlines, standards, outcomes, and assessments driving decision-making. But when you're leading a homeschool cooperative or microschool that serves trauma-impacted learners, the crown belongs somewhere else:

Regulation first. Rigor second. Every time.

Trauma does not just live in memory. It lives in the nervous system. Until that system feels safe, no amount of worksheets, lesson plans, or "just try harder" speeches will work.

WHAT IS REGULATION?

Regulation is a person's ability to manage their emotional and physical state in response to stress or stimulation.

In kids, regulation looks like:

- Being able to focus and shift attention

- Managing frustration or disappointment without melting down

- Recovering from upset without shutting down completely

- Asking for help or support when overwhelmed

For trauma-impacted learners, regulation is often fragile or missing altogether. Their brains have been trained to survive, not to sit still and solve equations.

So our job isn't to punish dysregulation. It's to help them practice regulation.

HOW TRAUMA DISRUPTS REGULATION

When a student has experienced trauma, especially ongoing or complex trauma, their nervous system is stuck on high alert. They live in what we call **"survival mode,"** constantly scanning for danger, expecting rejection, or reacting disproportionately to minor stressors.

That might look like:

- Bursting into tears over a math problem

- Shutting down after a transition

- Yelling when corrected

- Walking out when asked to try again

They're not being difficult. Their brain is doing exactly what it was wired to do: protect them.

We cannot teach over that. We have to teach *through* it.

SIGNS A STUDENT IS DYSREGULATED

Sometimes dysregulation looks loud and aggressive. Other times, it's quiet and masked.

Here's what to watch for:

- Fidgeting, pacing, or constant movement
- Sudden silence or lack of eye contact
- Sarcasm, defiance, or blaming
- Repetitive questions or obsessive thinking
- Physical complaints (headache, stomachache, fatigue)
- Inability to start or complete tasks

Instead of asking, "Why won't they do the work?"

Ask, "Is their brain ready to learn right now?"

If the answer is no, regulate first.

CO-REGULATION: THE SECRET SAUCE

You know what no one tells educators?

Regulation is contagious.

When you're calm, grounded, and steady, you create a nervous system that students can borrow.

That's called co-regulation and it's one of your most powerful tools.

Ways to co-regulate:

- Speak in a slow, even tone
- Offer grounding statements: "You're safe. I'm not upset. Let's slow down."
- Mirror calm breathing
- Sit beside them, not across from them
- Validate the emotion before correcting behavior

"You look overwhelmed. Let's take a few deep breaths together and figure it out after."

"You don't have to fix this alone. I'm here with you."

BUILDING REGULATION INTO YOUR ROUTINE

In trauma-informed homeschool spaces, regulation is not a response. It is a rhythm.

It's part of how you design the *whole day*.

Here's how:

Morning: Set the Tone

- Start with music, movement, or mindfulness

- Use check-ins: "What color is your mood today?"

- Invite students to name a goal and a need

Midday: Keep the Body Moving

- Include brain breaks or sensory walks

- Offer movement-based learning (use sidewalk chalk for math, hopscotch for spelling)

- Create flexible seating and posture options

Afternoon: Reflect and Regroup

- End with a calming activity (journaling, art, group gratitude)

- Acknowledge emotions that showed up during the day

- Let students help co-create next day's plan (this builds control and predictability)

ACADEMIC RIGOR *WITHOUT* EMOTIONAL READINESS IS EDUCATIONAL HARM

This might be hard to hear, but it needs to be said:

If you are pushing a child to meet grade-level standards while ignoring their nervous system's cry for help, you are not educating them. You are retraumatizing them.

Academic goals are important. But they are not *more important* than emotional safety.

When a student is regulated, the entire learning process shifts.

Retention improves, focus sharpens, and confidence rises. You don't need to sacrifice rigor. You just need to sequence it after regulation.

WHAT ABOUT THE HIGH-ACHIEVING, DYSREGULATED STUDENT?

Not all trauma-impacted students struggle with grades. Some overperform.

They get A's. They say "yes" to everything. They seem "fine."

But inside? They're flooded. Numb. Burned out.

PAY ATTENTION TO:

- Perfectionism
- Fear of failure
- Exhaustion or chronic physical complaints
- Obsessive productivity

Regulation isn't just for the kids who act out.

It's for the kids who *disappear behind their achievements*, too.

REGULATE FIRST. TEACH SECOND. ALWAYS.

You are not falling behind when you stop to breathe.

You are not wasting time when you help a student find calm.

You are not lowering standards when you prioritize nervous system safety.

You are teaching the most important skill a child can carry into the world:

- How to stay in their body when the world feels unsafe.

- How to listen to their needs before they erupt.

- How to stay present long enough to learn.

This is not soft teaching. This is revolutionary teaching.

Because when we regulate before we rigor—we don't just improve outcomes.

We change lives.

Regulation is not just for elementary students. Middle and high school students need it as well. In fact, the older the learner, the more layered their stress responses can become. Many teens, and even adult students, are carrying unresolved trauma, heightened academic pressures, and complex emotional landscapes that can easily overwhelm their capacity to focus, connect, or learn. Regulation at the upper grade levels doesn't have to look like coloring sheets or quiet corners (though it can); instead, it might be structured movement breaks, digital mood check-ins, mindfulness routines, passion projects, peer support circles, or time for creative expression. For these learners, regulation is about creating a rhythm of the day that builds in decompression, reflection, and restoration—because brains of all ages learn best when they feel safe, seen, and steady.

REGULATION FIRST: DAILY RHYTHM FOR MIDDLE & HIGH SCHOOL STUDENTS

This daily rhythm is designed to prioritize regulation, emotional wellness, and relational safety while still maintaining academic structure for middle and high school students. Use this as a visual guide to plan a trauma-informed day that begins and ends with connection.

1. Arrival + Connection Check-In

Students begin their day with a non-academic check-in. This could include a brief one-on-one chat, an emotion color chart, or a group pulse check.

2. Grounding Activity

A short, shared moment that regulates the nervous system. Options include breathing exercises, guided meditation, or low-stimulation movement like stretching.

3. Learning Block #1 (Focused Academic Time)

Begin structured academic instruction, keeping expectations clear and pacing predictable and offering choices when possible..

4. Regulation Break

Mid-morning break that includes snacks, hydration, movement, or sensory input. This is not a reward; it's part of learning.

5. Learning Block #2 (Group or Project-Based Learning)

Continue academic work in a more interactive format: group discussions, hands-on projects, or technology-integrated lessons.

6. Emotional Check-In + Reflection

Pause to reflect on the day through journaling, open dialogue, or quiet activities. Create space for students to name their feelings and needs.

7. Creative/Exploratory Time

Allow time for passion projects, artistic expression, student-led learning, or curiosity-driven exploration.

8. Community Wrap-Up

End the day together with affirmations, appreciations, and a preview of what's next. Reinforce that school is a safe space to return to.

SAMPLE WRAP-UP AFFIRMATIONS

"I did the best I could today, and that is enough."

"Whatever I didn't finish today, I can try again tomorrow."

"It's okay to feel tired. Rest helps me grow stronger."

"I am proud of myself for showing up, even when it was hard."

"My emotions are valid, and they do not define my worth."

"I am learning how to handle challenges with more strength each day."

Chapter 9

WHEN CRISIS COMES

A TRAUMA-INFORMED RESPONSE PLAN FOR HOMES-CHOOL SPACES

"You do not rise to the level of your training in a crisis. You fall to the level of your systems. If you do not have a response plan, your reaction becomes the plan." —Dr. Annise Mabry

Let me say this right now:

Crisis will come.

Not if—when.

Someone will panic.

Someone will lash out.

Someone will disclose something that stops you in your tracks.

You will be standing there with no school resource officer, no trained social worker in the next office, and no counselor down the hall. It will be just you, a child in crisis, and a choice.

The time to build your trauma-informed response plan is before the storm, not during it.

This chapter will walk you through how to create a trauma-informed crisis response system specifically for homeschool cooperatives and microschools, one rooted in restoration, regulation, and relational safety.

WHAT COUNTS AS A CRISIS IN A HOMESCHOOL SETTING?

Crisis in our context doesn't always look like what public schools prepare for. We're not talking about active shooters or fire drills (though we should have a safety plan for those too).

In homeschool cooperatives and microschools, crisis often looks like:

- A student running out of the learning space or refusing to engage

- A full emotional breakdown (sobbing, screaming, or rage)

- Disclosure of abuse, neglect, self-harm, or suicidal thoughts

- A triggered parent who becomes aggressive or emotionally unstable

- A student exhibiting psychosis or severe mental health symptoms

- A caregiver's sudden death, arrest, or crisis that impacts the child

If a student's physical or emotional safety is compromised and your typical routines no longer work, you are in crisis mode.

THE FOUR R'S OF A TRAUMA-INFORMED CRISIS RESPONSE

When crisis hits, we fall back on what we've trained ourselves to do. That's why I use the Four R's model as the backbone of every homeschool cooperative crisis plan.

1. Recognize

Know the signs that something is escalating

Train your team to spot changes in tone, posture, voice, and language

Look for patterns of withdrawal, sudden agitation, or confusion

Your script: "I'm noticing you're having a hard time. You don't have to do this alone."

2. Regulate

Before you do anything else, help the student return to safety

Remove them from overstimulating environments if needed

Go to your regulation corner or mental wellness room

Use a calm tone, non-threatening posture, and slow your own breathing

Your script: "Let's name five things you see. Now four things you can touch…"

3. Relate

After the student is calm, begin restoring connection

Validate their emotions without interrogating them

Use relational language that reinforces safety and belonging

Your script: "That was a really big moment. You are not in trouble. I am here, and we will work through it."

4. Restore

Only after regulation and relationship has been re-established should you address what happened

Focus on repair, not punishment

Collaborate on how to prevent or handle similar moments in the future

Your script: "What do you wish had gone differently?" "Let's come up with a plan together so next time, you have more support."

ROLES AND RESPONSIBILITIES DURING A CRISIS

Every co-op, no matter how small, needs a clearly outlined team response plan. Don't wait until emotions are high and the room is loud to figure out who does what.

Here's what that might look like:

ROLE	RESPONSIBILITY
Lead Educator/Facilitator	De-escalates student and initiates regulation response
Support Staff or Parent Volunteer	Clears the space of other students, protects dignity, ensures physical safety
Designated Family Liaison	Communicates with caregiver post-incident in calm, non-blaming manner
Documentation Lead	Records what happened using neutral, factual language

Pro Tip: Practice role-playing crisis responses during staff meetings or parent training sessions. If you don't train the nervous system, it won't show up the way you need it to.

CREATING A WRITTEN CRISIS PROTOCOL

A trauma-informed homeschool crisis response plan should include:

- Incident Types: Define which behaviors or events trigger crisis protocol.

- Step-by-Step Response: Detail the Four R's with scripts, tools, and actions.

- Designated Responders: Assign team members and back-ups for each role.

- Caregiver Communication Plan: Define how and when families are notified.

- After-Action Review: Establish a debrief process (within 24 hours) for the adult team.

- Restoration Pathway: Create a collaborative reintegration
  plan for the student.

Would you like a printable template for this? I can build one that matches your format and tone.

WHAT NOT TO DO IN A CRISIS

Sometimes the best trauma-informed support is knowing what not to do.

Don't threaten, bribe, or yell.

This only activates the survival brain further.

Don't isolate as punishment.

Offer quiet space, not banishment.

Don't try to teach in the middle of dysregulation.

Correction belongs after connection, not before.

Don't involve law enforcement unless safety is at immediate risk.

Calling the police on a child in crisis can cause irreparable harm.

HEALING AFTER THE STORM

Crisis doesn't have to leave scars. When handled with intention, it can build trust, confidence, and even deeper relationships.

After a crisis:

- Reassure the child: "You're still a part of this community. You still belong here."

- Reassure the family: "We're not calling to blame—we're calling to support."

- Reassure the team: "We don't have to be perfect. We just have to keep showing up regulated."

If you're doing this work right, a child can have the worst day of their life in your co-op—and still leave feeling seen, held, and whole.

CHAPTER REFLECTION: CRISIS HAPPENS—NOW WHAT?

Ask yourself and your team:

- Do we have a plan for emotional and behavioral crises?

- Who handles regulation? Who manages communication?

- Are students part of creating their own restoration plans?

- How do we debrief not just what happened, but how we handled it?

How you respond to crisis does not just define your homeschool culture. It defines what your students believe about themselves after everything falls apart.

Chapter 10
SUSTAINING THE WORK

ADVOCACY, POLICY, AND LONG-TERM IMPACT

"It is one thing to teach trauma-informed practices. It is another to lead them, live them, and legislate them. If we want systems to change, we have to take our stories to the decision-making table."
—Dr. Annise Mabry"

Let's be real, trauma-informed teaching doesn't just belong in a workbook, a one-day training, or a Pinterest board. It belongs in policy. In funding. In the future of how we define education itself.

If you've come this far, if you've committed to building a homeschool cooperative or microschool where healing isn't just a side benefit but the *foundation* you already know this work is bigger than you.
The question is: how do we keep it going? How do we protect it, grow it, and push it into spaces that still think trauma-informed means soft, unstructured, or optional?

This chapter is your blueprint for sustainability, financially, emotionally, structurally, and systemically. This is not a feel-good trend. It is a movement. We are no longer asking permission.

PERSONAL SUSTAINABILITY – THE WORK CAN'T THRIVE IF YOU'RE BURNED OUT

Let's start here because no one else will say it:

You can't sustain a trauma-informed model if you're running on fumes.

You are a leader.

You are also a human being.

Trauma-informed teaching without trauma-informed living is a fast track to compassion fatigue and collapse. And I've lived that. I've hit the wall. I've cried between lessons. I've considered walking away.

So here's what I want you to build into your own life as a sustainability strategy:

- **A regulated daily rhythm** that includes breath, silence, or joy
- **Office hours** (yes, even if you run a co-op out of your living room)
- **Boundaries around availability** to protect your mental health
- **A peer circle or advisory board** that pours back into you
- **Scheduled rest and restoration weeks** that are sacred and non-negotiable

Because your nervous system is part of your curriculum.
If you're dysregulated, overworked, and invisible, your students will feel that, no matter how beautifully your lesson plan is typed up.

PROGRAM SUSTAINABILITY – FUNDING WHAT MATTERS WITHOUT LOSING YOUR WHY

Let's talk money.

The truth is, many trauma-informed homeschool programs start with passion and burn out from poverty.

You can't sustain this work on love and grit alone.

You need a funding model that aligns with your mission, not exploits your mission.

WAYS TO FUND A TRAUMA-INFORMED HOMESCHOOL PROGRAM:

Method	Pro Tips
Sliding scale tuition	Normalize access over affordability. Offer tiers, but define minimums.
Local partnerships	Mental health agencies, juvenile justice, or workforce development grants.
Grant funding	Look beyond education grants—apply under health, mental wellness, or community impact.
Affiliate programs	Partner with curriculum providers or trauma-informed resource creators.
Service-based income	Offer professional development, evaluation, or consulting to other programs.

Your program deserves to be funded.

Not because it's flashy. Not because it's popular.

Because it's effective, and every time a child graduates with dignity, you prove it.

POLICY INFLUENCE – MAKING TRAUMA-INFORMED PRACTICE A RIGHT, NOT A PRIVILEGE

Now let's talk systems.

The reason so many families find their way to homeschool is because the system failed them. Here is the truth. You are not just fixing the fallout. You are creating a new model. That work makes you an advocate, whether you asked to be or not.

So let's put your experience to work in these key areas:

POLICY PRIORITIES FOR TRAUMA-INFORMED HOMES-CHOOL EDUCATION

1. **Funding equity for alternative education programs**

   Advocate for trauma-informed homeschool and microschool models to qualify for state-level scholarship and intervention funding (like Georgia's Promise Scholarship).

2. **Trauma-informed training requirements for cooperative leaders**

   Push for trauma-informed certification or baseline professional development to ensure consistency and quality.

3. **Inclusive accountability standards**

   Reject standardized test-only models. Promote portfolio assessments, competency-based evaluations, and project-based graduation pathways.

4. **Interagency collaboration**

   Work with departments of juvenile justice, foster care, and public health to embed education access into service plans.

5. **Recognition of homeschool graduates in workforce pipelines**

   Demand equal opportunity access to jobs, college enrollment, and technical credentials for homeschool graduates.

You don't have to do this alone.

Get loud with school board members, legislators, advocacy coalitions. Your co-op is proof of concept. Now it's time to take it to the people with power.

LEGACY PLANNING – WHAT HAPPENS AFTER YOU?

You built something beautiful.

Now let's make sure it doesn't live and die with you.

Ask yourself:

- What happens if I step away for three months?

- Who else knows how to run this program?

- What is documented and what lives only in my brain?

- What's the long-term vision and who's trained to carry it forward?

Legacy Actions You Can Take Today:

- Create a standard operating manual (daily rhythms, academic pacing, crisis response)

- Build an advisory team or board with leadership potential

- Develop a parent training or apprenticeship model for new facilitators

- Start recording your systems—on video, in journals, or in community binders

- License your model to other leaders in rural or trauma-impacted communities

Because real sustainability means that when you rest, the movement doesn't fall apart. It rises in your absence.

FROM RESTORATIVE TO REVOLUTIONARY

If you've made it to this chapter, I want to tell you this:

You are not just a trauma-informed educator.

You are a movement-builder.

A policy shifter.

A story rewriter.

A liberator in a system that was never built for our children to thrive.

Your homeschool cooperative, your microschool, and your kitchen table classroom are sites of resistance. Every time a student walks in dysregulated and walks out restored, you are doing more than education.

You're doing revolution.

Now sustain it.

Fund it.

Protect it.

Pass it on.

Healing should not end with one classroom. It should echo into a generation.

# Chapter 11
THE EDUCATOR'S HEALING JOURNEY

"You can't teach restoration if you don't know how to receive it. You can't hold space for healing if you don't give yourself permission to be whole." —Dr. Annise Mabry"

Let's talk about the part no one wants to say out loud.

You can have the most trauma-informed classroom. The best regulation routines. The softest tone. The strongest curriculum.

You can still be breaking inside.

You can be the one everyone turns to and still feel like there is no one holding you.

You can be surrounded by children who are finally healing and still grieve the parts of yourself that never had that chance.

This chapter is not about your students. It's about you.

You are not a machine. You are not a superhero.

You are a human being doing sacred work in systems that were not built for your softness, your fire, or your calling.

So let's take off the cape and breathe.

Let's breathe.

TEACHING THROUGH THE TRAUMA YOU CARRY

If you have chosen this work, chances are this work chose you first.

Many of us didn't just wake up one day and say, "I want to lead a trauma-informed homeschool program."

We became educators because someone failed us.

We created these spaces because no one created them for our children.

We chose restoration because we knew what it felt like to survive without it.

But that means we are often teaching through the very pain we've never fully named.

We carry the grief of lost dreams.

The weight of systemic harm.

The exhaustion of being "the strong one" for too long.

If we are not careful, unprocessed pain will shape our leadership. It can make us reactive, perfectionistic, or overextended. It can turn our classrooms into mirrors of our own internal chaos.

Healing is not optional for us. It is urgent.

SIGNS YOUR NERVOUS SYSTEM IS CRYING OUT

We're so good at spotting dysregulation in our students, but how often do we spot it in ourselves?

Ask yourself:

- Do I feel constantly on edge, like I can't ever rest?

- Do I snap at small things, then shame myself afterward?

- Do I struggle to separate my worth from my students' success?

- Do I feel guilt for resting, or anger for needing it?

- Do I fantasize about quitting… just so I can breathe?

These aren't failures.

These are flags. Your body is whispering what your spirit is afraid to admit: *You're tired. You need tending too.*

MINI SELF-ASSESSMENT CHECKLIST

Check the statements that apply to you:

- ❏ I have at least one day a week with no work responsibilities.
- ❏ I have a peer or mentor I can be emotionally honest with.
- ❏ I practice a daily calming or grounding activity.
- ❏ I recognize when I'm overwhelmed and take action to restore.
- ❏ I have systems in place so my work doesn't fall apart if I step away.

REFLECTION PROMPTS

- What parts of your story still need your attention?
- What would it look like for you to feel whole, outside of your role?
- How do you respond when someone offers you help or care?
- What boundaries would help you protect your peace?

CREATING A HEALING RHYTHM

You don't need a retreat in Bali to start healing (though wouldn't that be nice?).

You need small, intentional practices that bring your nervous system back into safety and presence.

Here's what I've learned works:

Morning Regulation (Before You Give to Others)

- 5 minutes of silence or stillness.

- Deep breathing with affirmations.

- A moment of gratitude (even if the only thing you're grateful for is breath).

Boundaries that Breathe

- Designate "no teaching" hours (even at home).

- Use an auto-reply or template to create emotional margin.

- Schedule your breaks the way you schedule your lessons.

Speak Kindly to Yourself

- Keep a "What I Did Right Today" list.

- Name your wins, even if they feel small.

- Speak to yourself like you would a child in crisis.

Permission to Pause

- Take a rest day even if the to-do list isn't finished.

- Delegate. Let good enough be good enough.

- Remember, rest is part of the revolution.

WHO'S HOLDING YOU?

We can't talk about healing without talking about community.

So many of us are surrounded by people, but feel completely alone.

Build your circle.

Not the one that praises your grind, but the one that holds your grief.

Find the one who says, "You don't have to do it all," and means it.

Let your healing be witnessed.

Let your tears be named.

Let yourself be held in the same way you've held everyone else.

YOU ARE WORTH THE RESTORATION YOU GIVE

This chapter is not about balance. It is about belonging.

Belonging to yourself.

Belonging to a life that does not require burnout to prove your value.

Belonging to a movement that honors the whole educator, not just the outcome.

Here is the truth.

You can't teach regulation from a place of dysregulation.

You can't model safety while your body is in survival mode.

You can't lead others toward healing while denying your own.

I will say it again.

You are worth the restoration you give.

Let this be the moment you come home to yourself.

Epilogue

RESTORATION IS THE WORK

I did not write this book from a place of arrival.

I wrote it from the middle of the storm.

When the grant funding disappeared, it did not just threaten the Tiers Free Homeschool Cooperative. It shook my faith in the systems that were supposed to believe in me. I had built a model that worked. I changed lives. I gave hope. I gave diplomas.

Yet in the eyes of funding institutions, I was still a small, rural, unconventional program that did not fit the mold.

That was my moment of clarity.

I was never meant to fit the mold.

Not fitting the mold is what shaped my methodology, defined my approach to sustainability, and anchored the legacy I am building for educators and families who were never meant to fit it either.

This book, this course, and this pivot are not about survival.

They are about liberation.

Liberation from needing validation from systems that never saw us.

Liberation from the burnout of being everything to everyone.

Liberation from the silence that too often keeps us from saying, "I am tired, and I do not know what is next."

If you have made it to this page, I want you to know something important.

Restoration is not the reward.

Restoration is the work.

The work is rebuilding after loss.

The work is pausing before you break.

The work is saying, "I am not okay, but I am still showing up."

This book is my restoration.

This course is my restoration.

This invitation to you is my restoration.

I did not have a road map.

I did have a responsibility to my students, to my community, and to myself.

I built while grieving.

I taught while tired.

I spoke while still healing.

You do not need to be perfect to be powerful.

You do not need all the answers to begin healing.

You do not need permission to pivot.

If this work gave you language, strategy, or even reassurance that you are not alone, then we have done something sacred together.

Keep building.

Keep teaching.

Most of all, keep restoring.

We are the movement.

We are the model.

We are the restoration.

Join me. Lead with me. Build this with me.

With love and solidarity,
Dr. Annise Mabry

Appendix A

REGULATION STATION CHECKLIST

A Regulation Station is a safe space designed to help students self-regulate, reset, and rejoin the learning environment with calm and clarity. Use this guide to create a trauma-informed area in your homeschool co-op or microschool that supports emotional regulation through sensory, physical, and visual calming strategies.

WHAT TO INCLUDE IN YOUR REGULATION STATION

Use the checklist below to stock your station with calming, sensory, and mindfulness tools.

- ❏ Sensory Tools
- ❏ Comfort Items
- ❏ Movement Options
- ❏ Mindfulness & Breathing Tools
- ❏ Creative Expression
- ❏ Visual Supports & Instructions

Visual Checklist

Use this visual checklist to organize your Regulation Station:

Appendix B

REGULATION STATION TOOLKIT

Purpose: To support emotional regulation through sensory, physical, and visual calming strategies.

SENSORY TOOLS

These help students soothe their nervous systems through tactile engagement:

- ❏ Fidget spinners or cubes
- ❏ Stress balls (varied textures like gel, foam, or sand-filled)
- ❏ Tactile strips (Velcro, sequins, or bumpy textures)
- ❏ Putty or therapeutic clay
- ❏ Weighted lap pad or small weighted blanket
- ❏ Noise-canceling headphones
- ❏ Aromatherapy roll-ons (lavender or citrus blends)
- ❏ Sensory bottles (glitter or floating objects in water)

COMFORT ITEMS

- ❏ Objects that promote emotional safety:
- ❏ Stuffed animals or plush toys

- ❏ Soft throw blanket
- ❏ Bean bag or floor cushion
- ❏ Hooded sweatshirt or oversized jacket for sensory security

MOVEMENT OPTIONS

- ❏ To support grounding and release nervous energy:
- ❏ Mini trampoline or wobble board
- ❏ Yoga mat or calming movement cards
- ❏ Stretch bands or resistance bands
- ❏ Wall push posters ("Do 5 strong pushes!")

MINDFULNESS & BREATHING TOOLS

- ❏ To center and refocus:
- ❏ Breathing ball (expandable sphere for visual breath practice)
- ❏ Pinwheel or feathers (practice slow breath by blowing)
- ❏ Glitter calming jars (watch until it settles)
- ❏ Guided breathing posters (e.g., "Smell the flower, blow out the candle")
- ❏ Mini sand timers or hourglasses (1–3 min options)

CREATIVE EXPRESSION

- ❏ For emotional release and non-verbal communication:
- ❏ Blank paper + coloring sheets
- ❏ Markers, crayons, or twistable colored pencils
- ❏ Water painting boards or no-mess doodle pads
- ❏ Journaling cards (e.g., "Today I feel…", "I wish someone knew…")

Visual Supports & Instructions

- ❏ Clear labels and steps to empower student use:
- ❏ "How Are You Feeling?" emotion check-in chart (with faces or emojis)
- ❏ "What Can I Try?" strategy menu (e.g., fidget, draw, breathe, stretch)
- ❏ "Steps to Reset" poster (1. Choose a tool, 2. Take 3 deep breaths, 3. Rejoin group when ready)
- ❏ "This Is a Safe Space" affirmation sign

Appendix C

RESTORATIVE LANGUAGE CHEAT SHEET

In trauma-informed and healing-centered spaces, the language we use shapes how students see themselves and their capacity to grow. Use this cheat sheet as a quick reference to shift from shame-based to restorative, strength-based communication.

FROM SHAME-BASED TO STRENGTH-BASED

INSTEAD OF THIS...	SAY THIS INSTEAD...
What's wrong with you?	What's going on for you right now?
You're making bad choices.	Let's figure out what support you need to make a better choice.
That's not how we act here.	That behavior doesn't match who you are in this community.
You need to calm down.	I'm here. Let's breathe together.
You're fine.	It's okay to feel what you're feeling. I've got you.

REFRAME THE NARRATIVE

Speak about behaviors, not identities. Reframe negative labels into observations and opportunities for support:

- Instead of "He's manipulative," say "He's trying to get his needs met in the only way he knows how."
- Instead of "She's lazy," say "She's overwhelmed and shut down."
- Instead of "They're attention-seeking," say "They're looking for connection."

RESTORATIVE RESPONSES IN REAL TIME

A student refuses to do work:

Traditional: "You're being disrespectful."

Restorative: "Looks like this assignment is feeling hard right now. Want to talk about it or take a break?"

A child pushes another:

Traditional: "We don't hit! Say you're sorry!"

Restorative: "Let's take a breath. Can you tell me what happened? Then we'll help you both repair this."

Teacher conversation with a parent:

Traditional: "Your child is disrupting the classroom."

Restorative: "We're seeing some behaviors that are signaling distress. Let's work together to figure out what your child needs."

TEACH RESTORATIVE LANGUAGE TO STUDENTS

Sentence starters and peer repair prompts:

- "I felt ___ when ___ happened."
- "Next time, I'll try to ___."
- "What do you need from me right now?"

When You Slip—Repair It

Even the best educators have human moments. What matters most is how you repair:

- "That wasn't the tone I meant to use. Let's try that again."
- "I was feeling overwhelmed. I'm sorry for how that came out."
- "You didn't deserve to be spoken to that way. Let's talk."

Final Reminder

Every word you speak is a seed. In your homeschool cooperative or microschool, plant restoration. Water it with care. Speak as if healing is possible, because it is.

Appendix D

CRISIS PROTOCOL TEMPLATE

This template provides a structured response for educators and staff in homeschool cooperatives or microschools to follow during a student-related crisis. Adapt the sections to reflect your specific community, resources, and roles.

1. CRISIS IDENTIFICATION

- Define the situation clearly and calmly.
- Identify the type of crisis:
    - Emotional or mental health breakdown
    - Physical health emergency
    - Behavioral escalation
    - Environmental/safety threat
    - Family/home-related crisis disclosure

2. IMMEDIATE RESPONSE STEPS

- Ensure the safety of the student and others.
- Assign a staff member to:
    - Remain with the student

- Alert the director or lead facilitator

- Clear or redirect other students if needed

- Call emergency services if safety is compromised

3. Regulation and Support

- Move the student to a calm, quiet area if possible.

- Offer regulation tools:

  - Breathing support (e.g., count-in breathing)

  - Sensory items or weighted objects

  - A calm, non-verbal adult presence

  - Allow silence before processing

4. Documentation

- Complete an incident report as soon as the situation stabilizes.

- Include:

  - Time, date, and location of the incident

  - Description of what occurred

  - Who was involved

  - Actions taken and by whom

  - Follow-up plan or referrals made

5. Parent/Caregiver Notification

- Inform the parent/caregiver as soon as possible.

- Use restorative language:

  - "We had a hard moment today, and I want to talk about how we can support your child moving forward."

- Avoid assigning blame. Focus on shared care and next steps.

6. Post-Crisis Debrief

- Schedule a team debrief:
  - What went well?
  - What could be improved?
  - Are additional supports or referrals needed?
  - Who needs follow-up support (student, staff, parent)?

7. Ongoing Support Plan

- Develop a plan with input from staff, caregivers, and (if appropriate) the student.
- Plan may include:
  - Check-in schedule
  - Trusted adult assignment
  - Modifications or accommodations
  - Referrals to external services

Appendix E

HOW TO START POLICY CONVER-SATIONS IN YOUR STATE

This one-page guide is designed to help trauma-informed educators and homeschool leaders begin advocacy conversations with local and state policymakers. Your lived experience and program outcomes are powerful tools for systemic change.

1. KNOW YOUR STORY

- What problem did your program solve?

- What systems failed the families you serve?

- How has your co-op or microschool restored access, safety, or outcomes?

- Tip: Prepare a 2-minute impact story you can share with any official.

2. IDENTIFY THE RIGHT PEOPLE

- School board members

- State representatives and education committee members

- State homeschool associations or task forces

- Local education policy advocates and coalitions

3. Request a Meeting

Use email or phone to request a 15–30 minute meeting. Keep it brief and professional.

Sample script:

"Hello, my name is [Your Name], and I run a trauma-informed homeschool program serving [Community]. I'd love to share some of our impact and discuss how policy could better support students like ours. Do you have 20 minutes to connect?"

4. Prepare Your Ask

Be specific about what you want. Examples:

- Include trauma-informed co-ops in funding opportunities
- Support nontraditional graduation pathways
- Recognize homeschool graduates in workforce programs

5. Follow Up and Build Relationships

- Send a thank-you note
- Offer to provide additional info or testimony
- Stay connected as legislation evolves

Remember: Policy change is a long game—but your voice makes it possible.